I Woke Up This Morning…

by

Keith Barker

Published in 2022 by FeedARead.com Publishing

Dedicated, with love and gratitude, to my wife, Diana, for whom this sonnet, describing the night we first met, 11th September 1964, was written.

Love at First Sight

A Roman soldier raised his eyes and saw
The dark night sky in all its majesty,
With stars extending to infinity,
And, as he had done many times before,
He traced the constellations he could draw
From stories in his own mythology,
Learned in his childhood days in Tuscany
Before he left his home to go to war.

And now, two English lovers, met tonight,
In this same Roman city by the Dee,
Gaze, as the soldier did, at stars above
And he, keen to impress her, will recite
His little knowledge of astronomy,
And by this show of learning win her love.

Acknowledgements

To my fellow members of the
Borderliners Writing Group
For their support and encouragement.

Contents

Thought for the day   7
Disappointed Dan   8
A Valentine Villanelle   10
Literary criticism   11
Sonnet Number 18a   12
The next Pope   13
The Cat   14.
Cords of Love   15
It's all in the Mind   16
Photography   18
Funeral for a Physicist   21
Footsteps   22
The Cat with Alzheimers   26
Lent Lament   28
To Steve   29
Santa's Staff Meeting   30
Pineapple Poll   32
Hunger   35
Respect   36
Rain   37
A Sergeant Major addresses his men   38
Brothers in Arms   40
A Writer's Lament   44
The Maggot   45
An Unexpected Present   46
To Hannah   51
Afon Ystrad   52

Childhood Games   54
A Strange Letter   56
Ellis Rides   61
A Buddhist Haiku   62
Vita Brevis   63
The Lazy Poet   64
Waiting for Godot   65
The Conjuring Trick   66
The Ballad of John Stilwell   72
To Joy   75
The Hunting Trip   76
The Fortune Teller   78
Limerick #1   81
Death on the Farm   82
Revenge is Sweet   86
Limerick #2   89
Daniel Kent – A Cautionary Tale   90
Confessions of a Bank Manager   92
Foreign Exchange   94
Tommy's Donkey   96
Limerick #3   101
One hour to Go   102
Beyond Endurance – A Sestina   104
Client   106
Who?   108
William Porter, who was disinclined to wash   110
Sid, who was inclined to be led astray   112
Linda, or the dangers of surgery they don't warn you
about   113

Thought for the day.

I woke up this morning with a bee in my bonnet.
Does anybody wannit?

Disappointed Dan

My name is disappointed Dan,
I am a disillusioned man,
The promise of my early youth
Was not fulfilled, to tell the truth.
Though blessed with some intelligence
I sadly lacked in common sense.
Mistakes I made were all repeated
And being utterly conceited,
I blamed the world for cheating me
Of fame, prestige, prosperity.
The accolades that were my due
Became infrequent and too few.
Life was not going to my plan
And I became a desperate Dan.

But then a flash of honesty,
The fault was not the world but me!
So, I became a different man
A cheerful, optimistic Dan.
It's such a wonderful relief
To moderate my self-belief,
And be content with what I've got
And that amounts to quite a lot.

This poem is ironical
And autobiographical
And so, I thought I should assume
A tantalising nom-de-plume.

My true identity is signed beneath.

I am

Yours most sincerely,

Keith

A Valentine Villanelle

If only we had met in France,
That land of love and food and wine,
Then maybe I'd have had a chance.

I would have asked you for a dance,
A favour you would not decline
If only we had met in France.

I would have held you in a trance,
My fingertips caressed your spine,
Then maybe I'd have had a chance.

It could have been a great romance
Like Harlequin and Columbine,
If only we had met in France.

If, from your many supplicants,
You'd picked me as your Valentine
Then maybe I'd have had a chance.

By sheer chance of circumstance
We met in Ashton-under-Lyne!
If only we had met in France,
Then maybe I'd have had a chance.

Literary Criticism.

I met an Australian writer
With antipodean attitudes.
His textbook on zoology
Was full of duck-billed platitudes

Sonnet Number 18a

Shall I compare thee to a winter's day?
Thou art more frigid, more inclined to freeze.
December winds do seem to round you play
As cold as from the Outer Hebrides.

Sometimes the winter climate is so cold
That even monkeys, cast in solid brass,
Their vital nether organs have to hold,
Lest some profound disaster come to pass.

But whether thou art frozen cold or not,
You always will arouse the heat in me,
And, though you might think I am not so hot,
Please let me warm you up to some degree.

If you'll not let me, then I'll have to quit
And leave you colder than a witch's tit.

(With apologies to Mr. William Shakespeare, although I think mine is better!)

The Next Pope

Some very sad news, the old Pope has died,
So, the bishops, in conclave, will have to decide,
Who is his successor to Rome's Holy See?
There are several contenders, so who will it be?
Bishop Neville is favourite some people say,
But several obstacles stand in his way.
Doctrinally radical, brimstone and fire –
But keep him away from the boys in the choir!
Bishop Jim so they say is next on the list,
He imbibes far too freely, is frequently pissed,
So that would appear to scupper his chances,
As well as the talk of illicit romances.
And finally, Horace, the man from Damascus,
Would be our selection if they were to ask us,
But sadly, they won't so we'll just have to wait,
In St. Peter's Square while the bishops debate,
And we'll finally know when they've got the right bloke
When we look at the chimney and shout, "Holy
Smoke."

The Cat.

Today I watched my next-door neighbour's cat
Invade my garden through a broken fence,
First moving stealthily, then lying flat,
Looking for prey with every muscle tense.

It seemed to me he used each feline sense
Locating every movement, every sound,
I watched the hunter, feeling the suspense
As he patrolled his latest hunting ground.

And then I knew a quarry had been found,
He froze and concentrated very hard,
Prepared to make a final killing bound,
And that is when I caught him off his guard;

A single, well-aimed kick up his backside
Saved a small thrush who would elsewise have died.

Cords of Love

Some things I trust will never fade,
And one of these must be our love.
It means it cannot be mislaid
A cord that binds us, glove to glove.

It's all in the mind.

People will tell you, "It's all in the mind,"
That the mind is the place "where it's at."
But if you reflect, I think you will find
It's more complicated than that.

Take for instance the case of a man with a pain,
That derives from a knife in his back,
"It's psychosomatic," they try to explain,
"You are just a hypo-chon-dri –ac."

"Somebody's just pierced my flesh with a knife,
The blood's coming out in great spurts,
And apart from the fact that it threatens my life
I can tell you it bloody well hurts".

"The pain that you feel is a safety device
That your mind hopes will teach you a lesson,
That sharp objects like knives are not very nice
In the hands of a skilful assassin."

"Likewise with the blood, that crimson red gore,
That you seem to think a disaster,
It's your mind's way of showing the wound to be sure
 It's the right place to stick on a plaster."
And then there's the mind of the inebriate
Whose imaginary manifestations
Cause the cerebral cortex to dissimulate
With phenomenal hallucinations.

16

Such as elephants, frequently airborne and pink,
Which is never their usual pigment,
An example that shows that an excess of drink
Can create such a frightening figment.

When faced with exactly this kind of delusion
A patient's physician once said,
"They are all in your mind, a fleeting illusion,
Just chase the things out of your head."

The patient decided this course should be tried
When a pachyderm charged into view,
"Go away, fiend," he cried, but sadly he died,
A real beast had escaped from the zoo.

The mind is a strange and a complex device
And to me there is not any doubt
How important it is to be very precise
What's inside it and what is without.

Photography

Photographs were invented in the Middle Ages by Leonardo da Vinci who was a genius and also invented helicopters, bicycles, false teeth and the Dyson vacuum cleaner.

Unfortunately, one day the husband of one of his models, Mr. Lisa, came to his studio unexpectedly and found out why his wife, Mona, was always smiling, so he punched Leonardo, broke his camera, and burned all his photographs. I think Leonardo invented pornography as well as photography.

So Leonardo gave up photography and instead he painted a picture of Mona Lisa which he hung in the loo where thousands of people come to see it every day so it must be really good.

After that, the secret of photography was lost for hundreds of years until in the Victorian times people like Lewis Carroll and Sherlock Holmes discovered it again. Lewis Carroll took photos of Alice in Wonderland who was a young girl that he knew. He took photos of her through the looking glass, which I think must be like a one-way mirror like they use in detective programmes. Sherlock Holmes took photos of fairies at the bottom of his garden, but some people said they were fakes and Sherlock Holmes didn't really take them it was somebody called Sir Arthur Conman Doyle.

In those days photographs were taken on glass plates, and I suppose they were like the plates they made when Prince Charles and Princess Diana got married. They are worth a lot of money now and sometimes get sold for 50p on Bargain Hunt or Flog It.

Then a man called Kodak invented film and a new camera called a box brownie because it was like a box, and it was brown. This meant that everybody could take photos of their family and scenery and especially their holidays, and they could take the film to Boots who would turn the film into photographs that you could show to people even if they didn't want to see them. Then when you were bored you could stick the photos in an album or a shoe box and never look at them again.

In those days all photographs were black and white except for some really old ones which were brown and white, which is weird. So it was impossible to tell what colour clothes people were wearing or what colour the scenery was, unless it had been snowing. Then somebody, it might have been Mr. Kodak again, invented colour film which was much more realistic and made people think how great their holidays had been even though they didn't think so when they were there. Colour photographs were more expensive so Boots were very happy about this.

In modern times, after I was born, they invented digital photographs and they were even easier because you could take them on your smartphone and watch them on your computer or print them at home. So you didn't need to go to Boots any more. To stop them going bust Boots became a chemist instead.

With digital photos you can take selfies of yourself and your friends and share them on social media like Facebook, Instagram and Snapchat. This is great because everyone can see what you look like and what you are doing. This is good if you are good-looking, and you are doing cool things. You can also use these photos to embarrass people or to blackmail them if they are not good-looking or doing bad things.

In the future I think we will have 3D moving photographs called holographs that will talk to you and you can put your hand through them like they were ghosts. I think this will be good because you can have all of your holograph friends at a party in your room and it wouldn't be crowded because you could just walk through them and you could turn them off if you got fed up, just like putting your old photos in a shoe box.

By Anthony Vole aged 13¾

Funeral for a Physicist

A top atomic physicist,
Abrasive and cantankerous,
Was hated by his colleagues,
Relations were quite rancorous.

So when at last he passed away
From a life that was unfriended,
Surprisingly his funeral
Was very well attended.

Scientists from every field
Came to his requiem,
And three of them read eulogies
Which seemed quite kind of them

But the content of those eulogies,
No words of praise or flattery,
Just hatred histrionic,
Verbal assault and battery.

The priest, when he made his closing remarks,
Reminded us all things must pass,
And this man passed as he would have wished
He achieved a critical mass.

Footsteps

Frank had felt uncomfortable for a few days;" Not quite himself," was how he described it to his wife, but he couldn't define it more precisely than that.

"It will pass," Jenny reassured him, "We all have our off days."

" I dare say you're right. I'll go for a walk, a bit of fresh air might clear my head."

"Watch your step then, there's been more snow in the night and it's probably a bit slippery under foot."

Frank pulled on his coat and opened the front door on to a snow-white landscape. At this hour of the morning nobody else had left a trace on the ground and he felt the magic he had felt as a child. His mood was lifting already and he set off on his walk.

He was enjoying the chill, fresh air, the snow lying on the bushes and tree branches the sound of his footsteps as they crunched through the fresh snow and into the frozen layers of yesterday's covering.

That was when he had the first inkling that something was not quite right. It seemed that the sound of his footsteps was ahead of the actual footfall.

"My hearing must be out," he thought, "some kind of auditory delay."

But no, the sound was ahead of the footsteps not lagging behind. He glanced down at his feet and saw two distinct footprints, a right foot, and a left foot, clearly impressed in the fresh snow in exactly the position he was about to place his own feet. Unable to stop, he carried on walking and each time he stepped into his own footprints, two fresh footprints appeared ahead of him, and for one insane moment he thought of King Wenceslas and his page treading in his footprints in the old carol.

He stopped, and the footprints stopped too, waiting for him.

Now he was worried! Literally frozen in his tracks, he decided to return home, he turned and began to walk back, carefully avoiding his earlier footprints.

He was relieved to see that his footprints were no longer appearing in front of him, but his relief was short lived as he heard behind him the sound of footsteps crunching in the snow as though someone were following him. Afraid to look back, but knowing that he must, he turned around. There was nobody there, but the phantom footprints were now two steps behind him, waiting for him to start walking again.

Frank's brain struggled to make sense of this situation. He could think of no rational explanation for surely there was none. He closed his eyes and took a series of deep breaths hoping to clear his head, and that when he re-opened his eyes, normality would be restored.

When he opened his eyes and looked over his shoulder. The footprints were still there, waiting, and above them the air seemed to be thickening and taking on substance. Feet exactly like his own were beginning to fill the air above the footprint, shod in boots identical to his own, and as the apparition grew upwards, he saw a perfect replica of himself materialising until it was complete. Frank raised his hand to his forehead and the apparition did so too. Frank began walking again and his other self followed him step for step.

Unable to stand it any longer Frank stopped and turned around, "Go to hell, whatever you are, leave me alone."

Seconds later the apparition turned and repeated Frank's words, in Frank's voice, to some unseen presence behind it. Convinced that either he or the world was going mad his head began to swim and his legs felt as though they could no longer support him. Afraid that he was going to collapse, Frank sat down where he stood and leaned back against the wall of a garden. Glancing to his left he saw that his other self was sitting next to him.

Exhausted, confused and terrified Frank closed his eyes and, though he was not a religious man, he prayed for this nightmare to end.

"Isn't that Frank over there?" Two of Frank's neighbours hurried across the road to see what was wrong with their friend. They found him stone cold and dead, sitting on the footpath which by now was trodden into a greyish brown slush with not a footprint in sight.

Later, whenever they talked about finding Frank dead, they always agreed that he looked as though he had his arm around somebody.

The Cat with Alzheimers

My cat appears to have Alzheimers."
"How do you know?" I hear you say,
The symptoms are as clear as day.

The cat flap confuses her,
Leaves her bemused,
Our corgi abuses her,
She just seems amused.

Mealtimes used to be night and morning at eight,
Now she cannot remember the last time she ate,
And every ten minutes she purrs round my feet
Suggesting she's hungry and simply must eat.

The birds in our garden go quite unmolested,
The sparrow, the thrush and the robin red breasted,
Hop around on the lawn without giving a thought
To the creature who once used to kill them for sport.

It's months since I found a dormouse on my doormat,
And they can't be extinct, I am quite sure of that
For out in the fields, they are breeding like rabbits
'Cos my cat has forsaken her mouse hunting habits

In search of some answers, I called up the vet,
He told me that pussies can sometimes forget,
But cases like mine were complex and rare
And in need of extensive, and expensive, care.

26

There was in his voice the trace of a thrill,
And his fountain pen scratched as he made out my bill.
"It's difficult to diagnose 'in absentia'
It's either Alzheimers or Feline Dementia

Lent Lament

A sinful local resident,
Worried that he was hell-bent,
Decided he would mend his ways
And keep it up for forty days,
Because it was the start of Lent
When people made a commitment
To give up things they'd always done
To make their lives a bit more fun.

He gave up booze and cigarettes,
And also, sweets and chocolates.
The betting shop was out of bounds
For bets on horses or on hounds.
It would have made him curse and swear,
But that had been replaced by prayer,
Finally, for the duration,
He also gave up fornication.

On Maundy Thursday sad to say
He gave up life and passed away.

To Steve

You and I have histories which we could well regret,
Things we have done, or left undone,
We wish we could forget.
But what is past can't be erased,
Today is all we have, this day the only one
That we can live and change ourselves
To new and better men,
Willing to make amends.
Who care for others, be a friend,
And knowing you
And knowing too
The place where you've come from,
I'm proud to know you and
To know the man that you've become

Santa's Staff Meeting.

All the elves and all the reindeer,
Santa Claus had called together
 "Something's got to change," he said,
"We can't go on like this for ever.

At last I've hit upon the answer,
Outsource the work without delay,
That would save us loads of money
The mums and dads will have to pay.

I've been in touch with Amazon
They're keen to have the work,
What they save on Corporation Tax
Will be an added perk.

Instead of sending notes to Santa
Kids can put their lists online
Amazon slaves will pack them up,
And all on unpaid overtime.

Deliveries will have to change
No midnight rides by reindeer sled
Just a constant whining noise
As drones go flying overhead.

I've done this job for far too long,
The going's getting tough,
I'm winding up the operation
I have had enough.

You elves, go into pantomime,
You reindeer, out to grass,
I'm going to the South of France
So you can kiss my ass!"

Pineapple Poll

There was a time, early in our marriage, when my wife decided that our social life was sadly lacking so I suggested that we join the Rock Ferry Amateur Operatic Society. This seemed like a good idea as my wife enjoyed singing, and I knew some of the members as I was once recruited to play a small part, "a common little drummer boy," in a production of The Gondoliers. I was about thirteen at the time, but I remembered it being an enjoyable experience.

So we went along to our first rehearsal and passed the auditions, in my case this was a great surprise as I have an awful singing voice, but I think they were short of men for the chorus.

We rehearsed our first show, "The Count of Luxemburg," and all was going well until the first night of the show. I went on stage in full costume and make up and as soon as the chorus began to sing the opening number, I opened my mouth, but nothing came out. So, I mimed the words for the rest of the week.

I decided that a singing career was not for me, but as it happened the Society's Stage Manager was leaving, and I volunteered to take on the job. I took my new role very seriously, read books from the library, made models of the sets, and built and painted the scenery for each show.

All went well for a number of shows and I'd like to think I was a good Stage Manager, a job I thoroughly enjoyed.

But then came Pineapple Poll! This is a short ballet based on the music of the Gilbert and Sullivan operettas. A local company of dancers were to perform the ballet as an interlude between acts of the main show.

The scene was set on the deck of a ship, something like HMS Pinafore. At one point in the ballet one of the dancers was to mime firing a canon which was part of the scenery. Most people would probably be satisfied by imitating the sound of the canon by a bang on the drum from the orchestra pit – but not me!

I did my research and found a theatrical supply company which sold explosive charges which could be detonated by touching their wires to the terminals of a battery. I could easily synchronise this with the ballet by watching from the wings.

However, the fire officer of the theatre insisted that the charge must be detonated in some kind of enclosure. We agreed that I would suspend the charges inside an old-fashioned galvanised iron dust bin, leading the wires out of the bin to the battery, ready for the charge to be triggered.

On the first night the result was spectacular, I timed the explosion to the action on stage There was an enormous explosion, amplified by the bin, and when the smoke cleared, I could see that the dustbin had been blown apart at the seams!

I'm pleased to say that the performance was not disrupted, and I was so pleased with the outcome that I decided to use the same method for the next five performances.

By the end of the week, I had destroyed six dustbins at no small cost to the Society, but all the members agreed it was well worth the expense.

Hunger

I'm starving and I've got a huge appetite,
I've had nothing to eat since supper last night.
Now I don't like complaining, but
My stomach thinks my throat's been cut

I could kill for a doughnut or chocolate éclair,
I could eat a child's arse through a cane-bottomed chair,
Or a steak from the bum of an old grizzly bear.
As long as it's seasoned and cooked medium rare.

So urgent is my nutritional need
That a scabby cat or a flock bed well-peed,
To my malnourished senses would seem
As tasty as Michelin three-star cuisine.

Give me dog food or cat food
Or old mousetrap cheese,
But feed me, feed me,
Somebody please!

Respect

Mr. Dennis Purcell,
Clerkenwell magistrate,
Observed a few moments of silence yesterday
Out of respect for a tramp
Who had appeared before him
Many times for being drunk

Finlay Nelson, 53,
had been found
dead
in a telephone kiosk.

SILENCE FOR TRAMP
Mr Dennis Purcell, Clerkenwell magistrate, observed a few moments of silence yesterday out of respect for a tramp who had appeared before him many times for being drunk. Finlay Nelson, 53, had been found dead in a telephone kiosk.

(I have carried this press cutting around in my wallet for more than 30 years. There but for fortune…)

36

Rain

Rain has potential; choose where it will fall,
And it will journey anywhere it may
To travel on as other waters call.

Then flows, determined, on its chosen way
Not looking back, as river or as stream,
Ripples and eddies all in disarray

Until it settles to a quieter theme
And rests awhile in some smooth placid lake,
Dormant and glassy, placid and serene.

But water moves, and soon it must forsake
This temporary respite on its course
And further downhill travels undertake.

But this time with a much diminished force,
And much more leisurely through meadows flows
Further and further from its mountain source.

And now its final resting place it knows,
The restless sea or ocean with its tide
Which neither knows nor cares which way it flows
But lets the moon and gravity decide.

A Sergeant Major Addresses his Men

Now men, you know that I worry about you,
As if you were my own flesh and blood,
So I sent a request to them up at HQ,
For a break from the bullets and mud,

And they've given us all forty-eight hours leave,
And moving us back to the rear,
And some other poor bastards will have to relieve
Us when we get the hell out of here.

It's a twenty-mile march to safety they say,
A place by the name of Arras,
So pack up your gear and we'll get under way,
We're leaving the shells and the gas.

Some words of advice, when we get where we're
going,
Steer clear of them mademoiselles,
And for all of the pleasures they seem to be showing
They're nothing but French Jezebels.

They are after your money, and that is a fact,
So the choices before you are clear,
You can just walk away with your virtue intact
Or with syphilis or gonorrhoea.

And try to stay clear of them frog's legs and snails,
There's a good chance you'll get diarrhoea,
And if you can imagine what that entails,
There's no toilet paper back 'ere!

We know that this war has no reason or rhyme,
But as soldiers, you're brave and you're skilled,
For a couple of days have a bloody good time,
Then we'll march back again to get killed.

Brothers in Arms

Christmas 1944, the sixth Christmas of the war, and the last. At least that's what the crew of Charlie Phillip's tank thought and hoped. They had fought through from the beaches of Normandy, driving the Germans back to the borders of their homeland and soon it would be over. Charlie, together with, Tommy Wills his gunner, Mike Riley his driver and Billy Knowles the ammunition loader had been together since they'd started training for the D-Day landings and so far, they'd come through it all unscathed. They were praying their luck would hold.

For the moment they were having a brief respite and enjoying a passable Christmas Day dinner put together by the cookhouse. It wasn't bad and with a few drinks and a singsong, letters, and cards from home, it was a good day. A break from the war. It wasn't to last.

News was coming through that the German counter attack in the Ardennes, which had started a few days earlier, was giving the Yanks up there a hard time. Billy Knowles seemed quite cheerful about it.

"I hope the Germans give them a good hiding," he said. "They arrive here two years late and spend all their time chattin' up our birds while we do the fightin'."

40

Billy had a very low opinion of Yanks since he'd come home on leave to find that his wife had been going out with one of them. In the fight that followed Billy had come off second best and his wife had gone back to her mother's. He reckoned she was still seeing the Yank.

The rest of the crew were quite happy that the Americans were at the front line, hopefully stopping the German advance and giving them a bit of a break. The Company Commander soon put them right on that.

"Get yourselves ready lads, we're on the move. We're going to help our gallant allies to knock seven bells out of the Germans. Refuel, get loaded with ammunition and be ready to move out at 0700 hours tomorrow."

Charlie kept the crew busy for the rest of the day getting their Churchill ready for a long drive and a tough fight at the end of it. It was a miserable journey over roads that were little more than churned up mud which had been frozen into rock hard ridges. Mike Riley had a hard time keeping the tank in a straight line and everyone on board was jolted and bounced around until they were sick of it. Whenever they could, they got off and walked beside the tank for a while, just for a bit of a break.

On the morning of the third day of the advance they began to pass American tanks and infantry heading

41

back in the opposite direction. The poor buggers looked as though they'd had a rough time; a lot of them were walking wounded, roughly bandaged with field dressings, helping each other along as best they could. Most of them weren't more than kids, 19 or 20 years old. Charlie and Tommy were having a break walking alongside the tank, and they had time to have a few words with the youngsters, trying to cheer them up and handing out a few fags.

Then their tank suddenly veered off the track and came to a standstill with one of its tracks broken. This looked like it could be a good reason to sit out the rest of this action and hitch a lift with the Americans back to safety but, when the Company Commander drew level with them, he ordered them to repair the track and catch up with the rest of the company as soon as they could.

This wasn't a popular decision and the repair involved heavy lifting and complicated manoeuvring of the tank, to drive off the broken track, repair it with the onboard spares and then drive the tank back on to the repaired track and reconnect it. By the time the repair was completed they were a couple of hours behind the rest of the company, but they had to press on.

With everybody on board except Billy, who decided to walk a little, the lone tank carried on along the road to the beleaguered town of Bastogne, still passing the stragglers of the retreating American troops.

A solitary battle-scarred American tank passed by and one of its crew, standing in the open hatch called out to Billy, "Good luck up there, we're glad to see ya!"

Billy jumped up on the side of the tank, took out a grenade, pulled out the pin and dropped it into the hatch of the tank. The youngster, who had called out, ducked back into the tank but he was too late to find the grenade and throw it out to safety. It exploded. The tank veered off the road belching smoke. None of the crew emerged from the wreckage.

Billy ran back to his own tank without another word and climbed aboard.

(This story was told to me by a fellow member of a writing group I belonged to. He swore he heard it from an old soldier who told him it was absolutely true. You may choose to believe it or not.)

A Writer's Lament

A writer's life is full of risks,
(And I don't mean just *****),
Fountain pens or cheap ball points
Cause havoc in your finger joints,
You may develop writer's cramp,
And, working with a puny lamp
On close-up work will strain your eyes,
And you will find that RSI's
Are serious risks for keyboard users.
(There are no winners, only losers!)
Long hours hunched over in your chair
Can cause lumbago to occur,
And, if that weren't enough to threaten us,
A pencil jab can give us tetanus!
Writing needs courage and endurance,
It's a wonder we can get insurance!

The Maggot.

From the killing field of Shiloh,
The wreckage of the shot and shell
Laid in rows on bloody trestles.
Was this hospital or hell?

Physicians watched my ministrations.
Patients, past their powers of healing,
Freed from gangrene, amputations,
They recorded, sought the meaning.

They saw me heal the broken flesh,
A crawling thing in fetid air,
Cleansing the necrotic wounds.
Self-preservation is my care.

Give me what I need to live,
And as I thrive, I'll make you sound,
Lucilia Sericata,
Healing in a bullet wound.

An Unexpected Present

It was my 13th birthday last week and I had a great time, lots of cards and presents including a new laptop from my mum and dad. Then my dad did a very strange thing, he gave me another present, wrapped up in fancy paper, and he said, "That's just from me," and he winked.

As I opened it I saw it was a book written by some woman called Hilary Belloc who I'd never heard of! It was called "Cautionary Tales for Children", and he'd written inside the cover, (in capital letters 'cause his handwriting is rubbish), "I WAS GIVEN THIS BOOK WHEN I WAS 13, I HOPE YOU FIND IT AS USEFUL AS I DID – LOVE DAD".

So I just said, "Thanks dad, I'll read it later in bed."

Which is what I did 'cause I knew he'd ask me if I liked it. Well anyway, the book was about all these stupid kids with weird names like Algernon or Godolphin or Hildebrand so it must have been written hundreds of years ago 'cause nobody's called Algernon or Hildebrand these days, at least not in my school. The thing about all these kids was that they had strange, annoying habits like eating little bits of string or slamming doors or doing other stuff that upset grown-ups, and these things always got them into trouble. In fact, mostly they wound up dead!

And the stories were all in poetry which rhymed but not like that William Wordsworth that we did in school all about daffodils and nature 'cause these stories were quite funny when you got to know them, and some of them made me laugh out loud. The pictures were quite funny too, but very old-fashioned.

But then I got to thinking, "Why has dad given me this?" but I fell asleep before I figured it out.

In the morning, after dad had gone to work, I asked my mum about the mysterious present. She said she didn't know about it until dad gave it to me and she hadn't had chance to ask him about it. She said she thought he might have been trying to tell me that I had some annoying habits that needed changing.

"Like what?" I said.

"Well, you are a bit untidy and he's always telling you off about that, and you do leave lights on when you're not in the room and he does moan about the electric bills, and you do slam the front door when you go out."

"So, you think he's having a go at me?"

"I'm afraid so."

"Well, I don't think that's a very nice birthday present, and anyway what about all the things he does wrong, that he gets away with, just 'cause he's a grown-up".

"Like what?"

"Well, you're always telling him off about wasting money on things we don't need, and not fixing things properly when you tell him to, and then having to waste even more money on getting a man in to fix them and that wastes even more money. And what about all the times he comes in late, or drunk or late and drunk, and I know he does 'cause I've heard you having rows. So, if anybody needs having a go it, it's him not me."

Mum frowned and I could see she was thinking that I had a point.

"Anyway," I said, "poetry can't be all that hard if that Hilary person could write it all those hundreds of years ago – and she was a woman! So, I'm going to write dad a poem and see how he likes it!"

"I think that's a great idea," mum said, "I look forward to reading it."

Actually, I don't think she believed I was going to do it, but I was, so I did.

That night, when dad came home, I told him and mum to sit down because I wanted to read them a poem, my poem, and this is it.

My father James, we call him Jim,
Has faults which do not trouble him,
They just make other people suffer,
Sometimes myself, but mainly mother.
And now, since I have read that book,
I think it's time to take a look
At things he does that drive us mad
But do not seem to bother dad.
He's not much good at DIY,
He shouldn't really even try.
For everything he does goes wrong
And then his language is so strong,
The air around him turns bright blue,
With words he didn't think I knew!
And then mum has to hire a bloke
To fix whatever has been broke.
At one thing dad is really ace,
That's getting "rat-arsed, off his face"
At least that's what my mother says
When he comes home in a drunken haze.
He has his good points, I'll confess,
Like helping maidens in distress,
That's one thing that I know for certain

Cause I saw him fix the bedroom curtains
For the pretty girl next door but one,
They closed quite well when he was done…

"That's enough for now," dad said, "we'll hear the rest another time. Here's a tenner to show how much I enjoyed it, now why don't you go to your room, your mum and me need to have a talk".

I could see from the look on mum's face that she definitely needed to talk, so I went to my room and listened to loud music on my new laptop with my headphones on.

To Hannah

I think perhaps that this is where our illness ends,
To know we're not alone
That others, that we had not known,
Reveal themselves to us as loving friends,
Who understand the depth of our despair
And know the damage which we must repair,
As our body, mind and, most of all, our spirit mends.
These friends, can understand us as no others can,
And with their help, example and their love.
We find recovery which brings the peace of mind
That we've been dreaming of.

Afon Ystrad

Prologue

This work is in two parts. The first part owes much to
the work and style of a Welsh poet Gwilym Ap Gonagall,
who felt that he was unappreciated in his native country
and so he moved to Scotland, changed his name to
William McGonagall and became famous as the worst
poet in the English language. It is important that this
work be read aloud in a Welsh accent.

The second part, a sonnet, is the more lyrical
component.

Part the first:

The Ystrad, as it flows through Wales
Is never mentioned in lofty tales.
For eight point eight three kilometres
It carries many thousand litres
And empties them into the Clwyd,
Quite unobserved by any Druid.
It is not eulogised by bards
At any of the Eisteddfods,
(The plural really is Eisteddfodau,
Which doesn't rhyme, and that is why
I bent the facts to suit my rhyme,
A thing I do from time to time).

52

But, I digress, it's not surprising,
Because I like soliloquising,
And writing in parentheses,
I'm off again – forgive me please.
And now on to my lyric theme,
About this unacknowledged stream.

Part the second:

A Sonnet to Afon Ystrad

As perfect as a stream can rightly be,
The Afon Ystrad makes its humble way
Along a bed carved through Clwydian clay.
Having no need of pomp nor majesty,
It simply flows within its chosen banks,
And does its job, and then it rests content,
Its waters in another river spent,
Asking no accolade, nor praise nor thanks.

And as I stand and watch it, I can feel
The tangled troubles of my life unwind.
The ripples soothe like balm of Gilead,
Their sound and movement have the power to heal,
And grant to me a welcome peace of mind
That flows to me from you Afon Ystrad.

Childhood Games

The games we played had many things in common
When I was growing up in Birkenhead,
There always were the goodies and the baddies,
And the baddies were the ones who wound up dead.

Those baddies were usually the Germans,
And, although we hadn't all lived through the blitz,
We ran around with arms stuck out like Spitfires
Shooting down the evil hordes of Messerschmitts.

On Saturdays we'd all go to the pictures
Cheering at the things our heroes did
By the time that we came out we all were film stars
Like Roy Rogers or perhaps the Cisco Kid.

Red Indians were shot down in their hundreds
Falling from their horses as they galloped by,
How would they find more Indians I wondered?
There was not an inexhaustible supply

Of Cherokees, Apaches and Comanches,
And when they ran out, as they most surely would
At some point in the not-too-distant future,
There'd be no more westerns made in Hollywood.

Still, we'd gallop to the park on our imaginary steeds,
Trying not to dwell too much on this disaster,
And we'd smack our bums in rhythm as we galloped on
our way
Because we knew it made them run much faster.

It's very strange to think that nearly all our childish
games,
Although we thought them innocent and thrilling,
Were not a good foundation for our future adult lives,
Based, as they were, on slaughtering and killing.

A Strange Letter

Opening the morning post in a small branch bank was one of the most boring jobs imaginable; nobody writes to a bank to say anything interesting. The usual routine was to slice open the flap of the envelope, with perhaps a cursory look at the stamp and post mark to see if it had come from anywhere interesting, quickly scan the contents to see whose pigeonhole it belonged in, shove it in said pigeonhole and move on to the next boring item.

There were occasional items which stirred the blood, and I remember seeing one envelope which bore the printed name of Her Majesty's Prison Walton on the front. It was addressed in a very childish scrawl to the Manager. We didn't often get letters from customers who were guests of Her Majesty; in fact, this is the only one I can recall, so I opened it with a keen sense of anticipation. Who was this villain? What was he inside for? What did he want? It was very interesting to say the least.

When I opened the envelope, the contents exceeded my expectations. Our correspondent was indeed a prisoner in Walton, and he was writing to us with a very interesting story. The writer, I can't remember his name, explained that when he was a baby, Rocky Marciano was visiting Liverpool. He was at that time World Heavyweight Boxing Champion, and his parents had asked him to be one of his godparents. Touched by this gesture, Mr. Marciano had placed a substantial deposit with our branch of the Bank for the benefit of his infant godson when he reached his majority. He now intended to visit us on his release from prison to claim his birth right, with the substantial accrued interest. He closed by suggesting that if we were unable to come up with his rightful inheritance the consequences would be immediate and probably violent.

My first reaction was astonishment followed by incredulity and amusement. Being but a small, letter-opening cog in the machinery of banking, I immediately showed this letter to my manager whose reactions were like my own. Nevertheless, banking being a somewhat more honourable profession in those days, I was instructed to make a diligent search through our ledgers to see whether any account existed in the name of the prisoner or of the renowned pugilist. The search, though thorough, failed to reveal any such account and we concluded that the letter was the work of a criminal whose past had ill-equipped him to carry out a fraud on this scale.

Bankers being naturally prudent people, (I refer you back to my earlier comments about the profession in those days) our manager referred the matter to our local head office and they, also being cautious in the light of the threat of violence, advised us to contact

Walton Prison to make further enquiries as to the provenance of the letter and the character of the writer. The manager retired to his office to make the necessary telephone call.

This had certainly brightened up an otherwise boring day and speculation was rife amongst my colleagues as to the outcome of the enquiry. When the manager emerged from his office, he told us that the writer was indeed a prisoner who had committed a series of minor crimes, none of them violent, and the advice of the prison was that we should ignore the letter and the prisoner would be warned against writing threatening letters in the future. Life, and banking, returned to normal and over the next days and weeks the letter was forgotten.

My job at the bank involved more than simply opening letters and during bank opening hours my main duties were as a cashier. I manned my till on one side of a wide mahogany counter and served our wide variety of customers, "with courtesy, accuracy and speed, and in that order," as specified in the cashier's training manual. There were in those days no bullet-proof glass screens to protect us from the customers, whose standards in those days were also higher.

In one particularly quiet period of business I saw a somewhat dishevelled man approach my till and, when I courteously asked if I could help, he said he wanted to see the manager. I asked his name and, when he replied, I immediately realised that this was Rocky Marciano's unlikely godson. I was alone on the counter at the time and so I turned around to speak to one of my colleagues behind the screen which separated the counter area from the rest of the office. As I did so I heard a scrambling sound from behind me and turned around to see that the man had jumped over the counter and had grabbed a bundle of £500 in one-pound notes from my till. Without even thinking, while he was still crouching down grabbing more money, I launched a kick which caught him in the middle of his chest and threw him on to his back a few feet away. By then two of my colleagues had rushed to my assistance and between the three of us we pinned him down and manhandled him into the manager's office to await the arrival of the police.

I remember feeling a little sorry for him as he sat in the office; he was a very small man, thin faced, with a prison pallor and he obviously had not thrived on an institutional diet. I don't recall him saying anything from when he gave me his name until he was led away by the police, seemingly accepting his fate as he had probably done in the past.

It was only when I went back to my till with a policeman to verify that nothing was missing that I noticed a short, wooden-handled knife lying on the floor where my attacker had landed. It had been sharpened to a vicious point and I think I came over a little queasy when I saw it.

My colleagues and I made statements to the police and there was some discussion as to what my attacker would be charged with. The law had only recently changed, and nobody seemed sure what the appropriate offence would be. The presence of the knife eventually determined that it was to be aggravated burglary, a far more serious crime than it might otherwise have been.

Later on in that rather exciting day I was called up to our local head office to meet representatives of the local board of directors. I received warm thanks and congratulations, many handshakes, and a cheque for £25 by way of a reward for my outstanding bravery. The Bank has always been generous to staff who put their lives on the line in defence of the Bank's assets! I frittered away this handsome reward on a reconditioned vacuum cleaner which served us well for a number of years.

As for Rocky Marciano's godson, I never heard any more of him. I assume he was returned to custody either at Walton or some other gaol where he would then have served out a longer sentence. I can only hope that during this period of imprisonment his outgoing mail was more closely monitored

Ellis Rides.

This is the moment.
You are moving away from me.
One small push and off you go.
The bike has stood in the shed
For months, still with its label,
"A present from Father Christmas".
I hold the label in my hand now.
One small push, you move away.
Will you fall or ride?
Ten, twenty, thirty yards,
You stop and turn around,
A smile of triumph on your face.
I smile back; you cannot see the tear,
I am so proud of you.

A Buddhist Haiku

Buddhists write haiku.
They don't do it all the time,
Only now and zen.

Vita Brevis

Life is much too short
To waste a single moment
Composing haiku.

The Lazy Poet.

There once was a poet, who said,
"I will do all my writing in bed."
But his blanket had faults,
He got 240 volts,
In the morning they found him quite dead.

Waiting for Godot

You should see this play,
You may like it or not,
There's no action to speak of, not much of a plot.
It's two guys waiting for their friend Godot,
But he doesn't turn up - the ignorant sod-o!

The Conjuring Trick

My wife, Julie, wandered into the room looking a little distant and ill at ease. Her mind was clearly elsewhere as I could tell by the fact that she stumbled over the cat and fell heavily against a Louis Quatorze escritoire which I had been saving up as provision for my retirement. Fortunately, no harm was done, as the cat left the room at a speed which appeared quite up to its normal pace and, upon examination, the escritoire had not been scratched or dented; they built well in the seventeenth century.

Turning my attention to my spouse, I noticed that she had a slight limp but, on the positive side, the stumble seemed to have shaken her out of her distraction and she was cursing at a level which I found reassuring as a sign of her recovered state of mind.

Taking her elbow, I guided her to a convenient seat and made more detailed enquiries about the state of her health, which she assured me was perfectly all right.

"Then what's troubling you? Tell me why you are not your usual jovial self?"

"It's the fact that I am growing old. In two months I will be sixty-five and I don't like it."

"But your age is one thing you can do nothing about, and sixty-five is a milestone not a gravestone! We should celebrate it. What would you like to do? A party, a holiday, a special birthday present? Anything your heart desires, within reason, just name it."

"Let me think about it," she said, "I'll get back to you when I've decided."

Two days later she did, "I'd like to go on a cruise," she said.

"But you've always said you'd never want to go on a cruise, didn't like to be penned up on a moving hotel with no chance of going outside."

"Well, I thought about a party and I had a vision of all our friends, with and without artificial hips and knees, trying to recapture their teenage years dancing to sixties music. I couldn't stand that, so a short cruise, a week or ten days would be better. I'll be happy with that."

"Leave it to me and I'll find something that will fit the bill."

So, I set out to find a suitable cruise and eventually found one that involved us flying to Rome, where we would stay for three days, then joining the cruise ship sailing from Civitavecchia for a seven day cruise taking in stops at Marseille, Barcelona, Majorca, Sardinia, Sicily and back to Rome.

Julie was delighted when she read the itinerary and started buying the extensive new wardrobe she would need for this ten day cruise.

We had a wonderful three days in Rome, taking in the sights, then a coach took us to the port of Civitavecchia and we had our first sight of the magnificent cruise ship that was to be our home for the next seven days. We were both staggered by the size of it, never having been this close to a floating palace before, and we couldn't wait to get on board and find our cabin. This took a little while to organise but we were very pleased with our cabin with its small balcony outside where we looked forward to sitting and watching the sea roll by on sunlit evenings.

***

At this point I will have to take over the narrative from my husband, Eddie, because when we had unpacked and set out to explore the ship, he slipped on one of the staircases and damaged his ankle. The ship's doctor examined him and decided that it was probably broken and would need a trip to hospital when we reached Marseille. In the short term he strapped it up, gave him painkillers and told him to rest in his cabin until we reached Marseille.

I was resigned to taking my first meal on board in our cabin but Eddie wouldn't hear of it. "You put on one of your new dresses and go to the restaurant, I'm sure you'll make friends."

Reluctantly, I agreed, and I left him reading in the cabin while I went and had what turned out to be a splendid meal. Just as Eddle had predicted I did make friends with two couples on our table and his accident was a major talking point. After the meal I told my new friends that I was going back to spend the rest of the evening in our cabin, but they protested that this was such a shame and, if Eddie was comfortable, I should come with them to the variety show in the main theatre.

I found Eddie almost asleep after his meal and another dose of painkillers, and he said he wouldn't mind at all if I went to the show as all wanted to do was sleep. So off I went.

I found my new friends in the theatre and we settled down at our table for a pleasant evening of entertainment. The acts, singers, dancers a comedian were very good and I was really enjoying myself, probably having drunk more wine than I should have!

The last act on the bill was a magician, I forget his name, but he was really good and when he got to the finale of his act he announced, "I am now going to saw a woman in half, can I have a volunteer from the audience."

Being near the stage and feeling really reckless I put my hand up and he came down and led me onto the stage. I regretted my decision almost immediately but as he led me up, he reassured me that he had done this hundreds of times before and it had never gone wrong.

On stage was a long wooden box and, with the help of the magician and his assistant, I climbed into it and lay down. As he was closing the lid he whispered to me that before the trick was performed I would be let off the hook and his assistant would take my place. That was a relief!

As he was fastening the padlocks on the box there was a tremendous bang and the whole ship lurched to one side, the lights went out and people were falling over and I could hear screaming as passengers rushed for the doors. The lights flickered on and off and I began to shout for somebody to get me out of the box but I could see that the magician and his assistant had already fled and, within a short time, I was on my own in the empty theatre, screaming to be heard above the noise of the metallic grating that filled the air.

By now I was in a complete panic. I knew that something serious had happened. A collision perhaps, I thought of the Titanic but there are no icebergs in the Mediterranean are there? Another ship perhaps, I just didn't know. I struggled to force the box open, but it was impossible. Was the ship going to sink? Was I going to drown? Nobody was coming for me, and I began to cry.

Then I realised that my new-found friends would be looking for me, they would tell them where to find me, I just had to wait.

It was the longest six hours of my life. That was how long it took for the search party to find me. I was the last survivor to be brought off the Costa Concordia: the captain, the magician and his assistant were amongst the first.

All this happened five years ago, and I am now approaching another significant birthday. This time I *will* be having a party, complete with sixties music, artificial hips and knees and definitely no magician!

The grounding of the Costa Concordia on the 13th of January 2012 was real, as was the fact that the captain was one of the first to leave the ship. The rest of the story is my imagination.

The Ballad of John Stilwell.

In the days when Parliament and King
Fought for control of the land,
John Stilwell was the preacher
In the Village of Nettlestand.

The squire of the village
Was a man of great renown,
He was Sir Richard Howard,
And he was for the Crown.

John Stilwell was a puritan,
And he took Cromwell's part,
Yet he allowed Sir Richard
Had a good and honest heart.

John stood one day with his verger,
Greeting his congregation,
When he saw two horsemen riding up,
With grim determination.

"We seek Sir Richard Howard," they said,
"We know he lives close by.
As he supports King Charles's cause
We mean that he should die."

"Good friends," said John, "you surely know
This is the Sabbath day,
And God will smile upon your work
If you pause with us to pray."

So, as he led them into church
John called the verger near,
"Go tell Sir Richard straight away
His enemies are here!"

"Tell him he must flee at once
With his wife and family,
And I will do the best I can
To keep these men with me."

Then John went to his pulpit
And opened the Good Book,
He saw the villains in their pew
And fixed them with a look.

He turned his eyes to heaven,
And summoned all his powers,
He intended that his sermon
Should last for many hours.

And so the Lord sustained him
And gave him greater strength,
His sermon was a wonder
Both in content and in length.

And when at last he finished
He sank down on the floor.
The assassins straightway left the church
And took to horse once more.

They galloped to the manor house
As hatred spurred them on;
John Stilwell had defeated them,
Their enemy was gone.

And so John Stilwell saved a man
With whom he disagreed,
May he be an example,
He did a holy deed.

To Joy

When I was on the path towards insanity or death,
There were so many places where I could have turned aside,
Where I appeared to have a choice.
But deep inside a powerful voice
Grew stronger and just would not be denied,
"It wasn't that bad," but, of course, it lied,
The memory of pain would fade; and then another lie,
"It will be different this time," the voice would cry.
It never was of course, except it was much worse.
The alcoholic curse of this most cruel disease
Is that it lies to us when honesty is what we need.
Ignore that voice and it will fade,
Confront it for the traitor that it represents,
It WAS that bad and NEVER will be different

The Hunting Trip

A group including Thomas Fripp,
Set out upon a hunting trip
To Canada's most frozen north.
They packed their kit and sallied forth.

They planned to shoot some polar bears
If they could catch them unawares.
Seals and walrus were fair game
They meant to kill them just the same.

As well as birds that might fly by,
Though penguins seemed in short supply.
The fact that penguins cannot fly
Was knowledge that had passed them by,
Likewise, the fact that, on the whole,
They're native to the Southern Pole.

They thought they'd live like eskimo
With igloos made from frozen snow.
To build them was beyond their wits
And so, the local Innuits
Were called upon to use their skill
While they looked on and drank Bovril.

And as the day drew to a close
The group prepared to seek repose.
Before retiring Thomas said,
"The one discomfort that I dread
Is being freezing cold in bed."
So, putting on his dressing gown,
Went out and shot an eiderdown.

The Fortune Teller

Strictly speaking she was not a Fortune Teller, just a person who thought she could see other people's futures and felt that they had a right to tell them what it was going to be.

Fortune Tellers, generally speaking, do not take any responsibility for the impact that their predictions may have on their subjects, nor do they hold themselves accountable for the accuracy of their forecasts.

Those who make a career of Fortune Telling are charlatans preying on the gullible, the vulnerable and the weak. You may cross their palms with silver, and sit across a table from them in a booth on a seaside pier while they gaze into a crystal ball, or deal out tarot cards. You may read your horoscope in a newspaper or magazine and pay no more than the cover price of the publication. These are commercial transactions, and the buyer has a responsibility to evaluate the quality of the product and act accordingly.

Despite their ludicrous claims and bogus credentials, these shysters are at least open about the fact that they are taking money and not responsibility.

Far more dangerous and potentially damaging are those people who gratuitously offer forecasts of the future to their family and friends.

Just as with the commercial Fortune Tellers these amateur soothsayers are fallible. They may be well-meaning or malicious, insightful, or well-informed, but their predictions need to be given and received with the greatest of caution.

When I was younger, probably in my late teens, I had my fortune told by my Auntie Glad, my Dad's sister who had taken me in when I was seven after my parent's marriage broke down.

My mother was a gentle soul who found it difficult to cope with the world, and she had mental health problems. This meant that she was admitted to the Deva Mental Hospital, near Chester, on a number of occasions either as a voluntary patient or committed under the Mental Health Act. I suspect that, in these more enlightened times, she would have been treated more humanely and probably made a full recovery.

I'm not sure what I had done wrong, but it had clearly been bad enough for Auntie Glad, the Fortune Teller in this story, to predict that I was going to make a mess of my life unless I changed.

The Fortune Teller's words were, "You'll end up in Deva, like your mother."

I can't remember what my immediate reaction was; I probably fought back or stormed out, but the words stuck with me, mainly because it was a cruel attack on my mother.

The Fortune Teller's words came true some years later when I found myself as a patient in the Deva

Hospital, the latest in a series of admissions to psychiatric units where I was treated for alcoholism.

As I sat in Newton Ward those words came back to me and, although they had turned out to be prophetic, they haunt me today as one of the most hurtful things that have ever been said to me; words I will never forget.

So, I will never be a Fortune Teller. I have no gift for seeing the future, my own or anyone else's. If I do give advice, I have to be aware of my own fallibility and consider the impact of my words on other people.

Limerick #1

On the motorway one poor old chap
Had a desperate need for a crap
His acute diarrhoea
Made him wish he was near
The Services at Watford Gap.

Death on the Farm

Detective Chief Inspector Hugh Dunnit sat at his desk and tried to read the notes in front of him by the feeble light of the 40-watt bulb over his head.

He had been appointed to head up the newly formed Rural, Agricultural, Non-recurring Crime Investigation Division, or RANCID, an appointment which he fully understood was a punishment for a series of failed investigations which he had recently overseen. He also understood that Chief Superintendent Patrick Thistle, a dour Scotsman, had taken a sadistic delight in choosing the name and acronym for the Division.

There were two manila folders in front of him, the staff files of the officers who were to make up his team. He was certain, without even opening the folders, that they would be others who had failed as spectacularly as he had.

The first file was for his second in command, Detective Sergeant Stanley Accrington. What a loser he was! If it weren't for the fact that his father played golf with the Chief Constable he would have been back in uniform and pounding the beat long ago However, as he grew up on a farm, his agricultural knowledge might come in handy.

Next up was Detective Constable Alex, short for Alexandra, Crewe. She was transferred to his new command from the Murder Squad. The main reason for this was that she had thrown up at so many murder scenes and post-mortems that pathologists refused to work with her. Hugh hoped that her new duties would not put too much of a strain on her obviously delicate digestive system.

These two sorry individuals were waiting for him on the other side of the door and were no doubt anxiously awaiting news of what their new duties were to be.

Well, Hugh said to himself, we may be a gang of losers but I'm going to show Patrick Thistle that he can't throw me on the scrap heap just yet. He was just about to go and give his new team a stirring speech to motivate them when, surprisingly, his 'phone rang.

"DCI Dunnit, Rural Crimes" he said.

It was the despatcher from Police Headquarters in Shrewsbury.

"We have a suspicious death, possibly a murder near you and the Chief Superintendent wants your team to respond and report back. It's at Belchers Farm which is only about three miles from you. The caller was Maggie Belcher and she's been told not to touch anything until you get there. A Crimes Scene Investigation team is on the way, but it will take them at least an hour to get there. Doug Deeper will be in charge.

Scarcely believing his luck, Hugh told the despatcher they were on their way and, pausing only to grab his mac, he rushed into the outer office.

"Right you two, we're in business. Potential homicide for our first case. Do you know Belcher's farm Stan?"

"Yes guv, it's only down the road."

"OK, you and Alex take the patrol car. Don't go near the crime scene until the CSI arrives, and don't let anybody else near. I'll follow in a couple of minutes in my own car."

When he arrived at the farm, Hugh was greeted with a scene that made his heart sink. Stan Accrington was busily and not very successfully trying to attach yellow and black crime scene tape to any object that stood still long enough. Alex Crewe was draped head first over a fence, her delicate stomach quite unable to cope with the sight of a dead body and the smell of the slurry.

Standing nearby was a stoutish lady surveying the scene and shaking her head in amazement.

84

Presumably this was Mrs Belcher and Hugh, ignoring his two colleagues, walked over to her. From her point of view, he could see the crime scene. In the middle of a slurry pond a body, probably male, was floating face down with a knife sticking out of his back.

"Mrs Belcher I presume, I'm Detective Chief Inspector Dunnit and I'm in charge of the investigation. Do you have any idea who the victim is?"

"Yes, he's been working here for a couple of months. He's from the Netherlands and he's here to study British farming methods. His name is Keest de Vrinj."

"So, what we have here is the slurry with de Vrinj on top"

Groans.

Apologies to everybody who has read this far in the hope of a far better ending than this.

85

Revenge is Sweet

I'm not a dog lover, and I can trace the reason for this back to my childhood when I lived with an auntie who, in my opinion, cared more about animals, particularly dogs, than she did about human beings.

In the 14 or so years I lived with her she had a succession of dogs; a cocker spaniel, a couple of chihuahuas and my particular enemy, a black and tan Pekingese which rejoiced in the name of Chung-Kee of Meech-Neena or Chunkie for short. Like many small dogs this one was snappy and bad tempered, especially towards me.

Chunkie was extremely finicky in his eating habits, and my auntie was always trying to find some new, tasty morsels to stimulate its appetite. I can remember it being fed on steak, on kidney and on sweetbreads and it turned its nose up at most of these dishes.

My auntie was afraid that her poor dog would starve to death and so she devised a novel strategy to get him to eat. When the food was put down and the dog sniffed, turned, and walked away, I was told to get down on all fours and pretend to eat from his bowl. This worked perfectly for, as soon as Chunkie saw that I was about to eat his dinner, he realised that it was delicious, and he began to attack me, yapping and snapping to chase me off.

My auntie was so pleased with this result that it became a regular ritual at the dog's mealtimes. I sometimes got a painful nip on my nose or ear if I didn't get out of Chunkie's way quickly enough, but my auntie thought this was a small price to pay if the dog was well fed. As you may imagine there developed a mutual hatred between me and the dog and, apart from mealtimes we avoided each other at all costs.

Is it any wonder that I came to hate that dog and I'm sure he hated me? He would often fly at my ankles if I walked past him, and I would give him a sly kick if I thought I could get away with it.

I was watching television one evening when my attention wandered to where Chunkie was lying in his usual resting under the sideboard. I noticed that he was chewing on something, and I realised that it was the flex of the table lamp which stood on the sideboard. The lamp was switched on and this presented me with an ethical dilemma; intervene or sit back and watch? I sat back and watched. It was not long before the dog's teeth penetrated the outer covering of the flex and reached the bare wire. The result was most gratifying; there was a bang, a flash and a sharp yelp. Chunkie flew across the room where he lay wild-eyed with his fur standing on end and a faint cloud of blue smoke hovering over him.

When the smoke cleared my auntie sprang to the dog's aid, picking him up and cradling him in her arms. He turned his head towards me and, as our eyes met, he snarled, and I winked.

Limerick #2

There was a young monk in Tibet,
Who fancied himself as a vet.
He caused quite a drama,
Castrating a Lama,
With one 'L' not two, for a bet.

Daniel Kent.

This is the tale of Daniel Kent
Whose love was to experiment.
At school he took up chemistry
The phials and flasks and formulae,
And chemicals and their reactions
For him were powerful attractions.

He took this fascination home
Where he could practice on his own
And upstairs, in an unused attic,
Made smells and bangs that were dramatic,
And then, creating work for vets,
Experimented on his pets!

Turning his attention to himself
He used the bottles from his shelf
To such effect he found he could,
Amend his mood, for bad or good.
Then, having tried out all his potions,
He craved to find some new emotions

He wanted something more exotic
And turned to substances narcotic,
And, just as could have been predicted,
He very soon became addicted
To heroin and crack cocaine
Which wrecked his body and his brain.

The moral of this tale is clear
I shouldn't need to state it here,
You'll end up like the other mugs
If you experiment with drugs.

Confessions of a Bank Manager

I once had a job,
a job where I had power,
The power of yes and no.
People who wanted money
asked me for it
and I said yes or no –
after due consideration of course.
And that was fine.
But sometimes
they wouldn't
or couldn't
pay the money back.
It wasn't my money
but I took it personally
and the job began to lose its appeal.

One day I sat in my office
and there, across the desk,
a woman cried.
Her husband was a comedian,
but she had nothing to laugh about,
the stand-up had fallen flat.
The laughter and the bookings
had dried up.
She couldn't pay,
and so she cried;
the tears of a clown's wife.

And I searched for words
and the words I found were the death knell for my job.
I heard myself say,
"Don't worry – it's only money."

Shortly after that
my employers,
with a rare flash of insight,
moved me to a job where my humanity
could do them no harm.

Foreign Exchange

As the bank I worked for believed in moving its staff around from time to time, at one point in my career, I found myself as a cashier in a small branch, near to the docks in a busy seaport. After a while I noticed that we were visited almost daily by a number of ladies who wanted to exchange foreign currency for sterling. The notes were usually US dollars or some more exotic, far eastern currency. For these more exotic currencies I had to ring up our International Branch to find out the exchange rate on the day.

Being at the time, young and rather naïve, I didn't realise who these ladies were until my manager told me that they were in fact prostitutes who plied their trade among the seamen from the ships in the docks. If they could not be paid in cash, they were happy to accept foreign currency which they brought to us to exchange.

Usually, this system worked well, and the ladies left the branch quite happy. However, on one occasion one of the prostitutes handed me a note that I did not recognise. It was very colourful, seemed authentic and on the face had a number followed by about six zeros. When I rang our International Branch for an exchange rate, they told me that it was worth about three shillings, fifteen pence in today's money, and any way they would not accept it.

When I told the "lady" this, she realised that she had provided her services, whatever they might have been, for free. She became very angry and used some of the most crude and colourful language I have ever heard. I was very glad to have a bandit proof screen between me and her and I was very relieved when she stormed out of the branch.

I don't know whether she ever met that seaman again, but, if she did, I'm sure she would have made him pay, one way or another, for his "freeby".

Tommy's Donkey

My story is about an Irishman called Tommy who came over to England to find work in the 1960's. He soon found a job as a labourer on the building of the M6 through Birmingham.

It was an ideal situation for Tommy; he was well paid for doing work which suited him down to the ground, requiring no intellectual input whatsoever. In his leisure time he would invariably be found in his local pub, The Red Lion, where the Guinness was good and there were always a crowd of his fellow countrymen to talk the night away. He was a popular member of the company, he told a good tale, made people laugh with his stories of "the old country" and always paid his way.

Although his general knowledge would never have got him onto the subs bench of even a mediocre quiz team he was acknowledged to be an expert on horses. He had grown up amongst them and knew their ways; he studied their form on the race track and he was more often a winner than a loser at his local bookies.

Tommy's dream was that one day he would win the football pools, then he would buy a thoroughbred racehorse which he could train to win races.

One Friday night, when Tommy was more than usually inebriated and full of good cheer, two new arrivals came into the pub. They immediately made themselves known to Tommy's company introducing themselves as Connor and Liam, travellers, originally from Donegal who had parked their caravan on waste land near to the pub. They were soon accepted into the crowd and, being travellers, immediately latched on to Tommy's love of horses which became the major topic of conversation.

When they learned of Tommy's ambition, they came up with an idea which they thought would please him.

"Thoroughbred racehorses cost a fortune," said Connor, "You'll never be able to buy one on a navvies' wages, and you haven't much chance of winning the pools, why don't you start with something a little less ambitious?"

Tommy was immediately intrigued, "What do you mean?"

"Well, horses and ponies may be out of your reach but how about a donkey? Donkeys are lovely creatures, very like horses in shape and temperament, and a lot easier to keep, and what's more I know where I can get you one this very night for £30."

Tommy was immediately impressed with this flawless logic but not being completely stupid, knew he should haggle over the price.

"I'll give you £20, but I'll need to see the beast."

"Nothing easier, come with us now and I'll introduce you to the animal and if you like him we can do the deal."

So, Connor and Liam, Tommy and two of his mates left the pub to inspect Tommy's donkey.

It was dark by the time they reached the travellers' caravan but, as promised, there was a grey donkey tethered to a stake on a grass verge. Tommy made a great show of inspecting the animal, whose name was Flinty, and with much talk of fetlocks and withers, pronounced himself satisfied. He passed over the money to Connor and was given the end of the rope which was attached to the donkey.

And so, the procession of Tommy, his donkey and his two friends Tim and Johnny set off walking through the streets of Birmingham to Tommy's digs. It had not yet occurred to them that they had no idea how Flinty was to be housed until Tim posed the question.

"Where are you going to keep him?"

"Well," said Tommy with the air of a man who had already figured this out, "I'll keep him in my digs for tonight and sort out something more permanent tomorrow."

"But your room is on the third floor," objected Tim.

"Did you not know that donkeys can climb stairs?" said Tommy with a confidence he didn't really feel, "you'll see when we get there."

Flinty apparently was not aware of his climbing ability, because when they dragged him through the front door and confronted him with the first flight of stairs, he sat down.

At this point Tim and Johnny were on the point of leaving Tommy to his problem, and it was only by appealing to their longstanding friendship, their obligation to help a fellow countryman in need, and the payment of £10 each that they were persuaded to help further.

"Right," said Tommy, "I'll grab the rope and pull him and you two get one each side of his arse and push him up."

Tim and Johnny were aware of the danger this might put them in should the donkey become so agitated that he lost control of his bodily functions, and it cost Tommy a further £10 each to indemnify them against such an event.

So began a battle that lasted almost an hour. The braying of the donkey, the cursing and swearing of the men and the clatter of hooves attracted an audience of Tommy's neighbours who overcame their initial annoyance at being roused from their beds, and stayed to cheer, some for the men others for the donkey.

Eventually they reached to door of Tommy's room; he opened it and the three friends dragged Flinty inside. Exhausted they all collapsed on the various items of furniture in the room with a great sigh of relief.

Flinty, who had not been used to excitement on this scale, cast a jaundiced eye around his new accommodation and, making a hasty decision to leave, galloped across the room, and leapt through the window in a manner that would have done credit to a thoroughbred steeplechaser. It did not take him long to realise his mistake; apart from the lacerations to his face and flanks, the drop on the landing side was breath-taking but short-lived. With an agonising cry that was neither equine nor human he plunged into a collection of galvanised iron dustbins.

Limerick #3

There was an old man of Prestatyn,
Who ate nothing unless it had fat in,
But it wasn't the grease
That caused his decease
But an overdose of Simvastatin

One Hour to Go

One hour to go, I have no fear,
And somehow this surprises me.
This artificial, calm veneer -
Barbiturates dissolved in tea-
Delivered surreptitiously,
This sense of unreality.

It's ten past seven, the minutes pass,
Emptying my hourglass.

They brought me to this cell last night,
I came in through that left hand door,
They locked and bolted it so tight
I will not leave through it I'm sure.
My exit door is on the right,
I'll go in peace, I will not fight.

And then at seven twenty-three,
The chaplain calls to bring me peace.
I think he needs it more than me,
 I see the anguish in his face.
He asks me would I like to pray;
I think he'll do it anyway.
"It's all the same to me," I say.

102

At ten to eight, the Governor drops in,
To say goodbye, there's no reprieve.
The chaplain, sadly, drops his chin
And wipes his tears with his sleeve.

My pain will soon be gone
But theirs will linger on
For justice must be done.

Five minutes left, I'm told to stand,
And handcuffs bind me, hand to hand.
I'm pushed towards that final door,
The chaplain, praying, walks before.

They place a bag upon my head,
I feel the noose around my neck
They tell me I will feel no pain,
But, if I do, well what the heck.

That's it, time's up, I'll have to go,
The trap door opens, cheerio!

Beyond Endurance – A Sestina

When we were married, in a carefree time,
We both believed our love would long endure,
And took the vow, "for better or for worse",
With little thought for how it might be tried.
We would be steadfast, never any doubt
To cloud the vision that was in our sight.

Maybe, had we been blessed with second sight,
We would have seen there'd come a troubled time,
But, if we'd seen it, I would have to doubt
If we'd have been more ready to endure
The ordeals under which our love was tried.
What started out as better came to worse.

Disease that kills love; nothing could be worse
Or more pernicious, lurking out of sight,
An enemy unseen which always tried
To overwhelm us, and there was a time
We almost lost the courage to endure.
For courage cannot long survive with doubt.

The only thing that seemed beyond all doubt,
Was that the future only held much worse,
And so it stretched, forever, out of sight,
Despair the last emotion to endure.
It seemed we would not stand the test of time,
Would be found wanting when our vows were tried.

104

There was one source of help we had not tried.
Could there be others who had shared this doubt?
We found there were and sought them out in time,
And found that some had suffered even worse.
They overcame our blindness, gave us sight
Of miracles and helped us to endure.

So over time we've managed to endure,
And so much more than that; each day we've tried
To keep our new-found happiness in sight,
For gratitude can always banish doubt.
And now we have the better, not the worse,
Exactly what we wanted all the time.

Because we've tried, we can without a doubt,
Enjoy the better and endure the worse,
And, for the future, keep in sight a more contented
time.

Client

*"A person who has made the customary choice
between the two methods of being legally robbed"*
        Ambrose Bierce – The Devil's Dictionary

I ask you to consider then
An earlier, simpler period when
Professionals had clients who
Would pay their fees when they were due,
And, whether they were small or large,
Raise not an eyebrow at the charge,
Considering that sound advice
Was worth the cost at any price.
These trusting fools would often find
That somebody would rob them blind,
And even clients more astute
Were separated from their loot
By scoundrels whose financial health
Was based on stealing others' wealth.

But not so in this present day,
We're more enlightened so they say.
Professional advice is free,
 Or so it would appear to be.
We do not need to leave our house
As with a keyboard and a mouse
The internet is our adviser,
But has it made us any wiser?
Or is it merely the road

To Information overload.
Websites sprouting in profusion
Only lead to more confusion,
And so, it's hard to make our choices
When hearing these conflicting voices.

Blind fools may often go astray
And so, get robbed along the way
But men can make the wrong decision
When blessed with twenty-twenty vision!

Who?

At one point in my career, I was appointed Operations Manager at a branch of the bank in the Northwest of England. It was my job to ensure that the branch ran smoothly, and all procedures were followed correctly.

We had a counter service where we had five or six cahiers to take care of the needs of our customers. Routine withdrawals by our own customers were fine if they had funds in their accounts. But, if a customer of another branch wanted to make a withdrawal, the transaction had to be referred to me unless the customer had a valid cheque guarantee card. This was even more important for large amounts.

On one occasion one of the cashiers came to me with a cheque for £500 drawn on another branch and he asked me would it be alright to cash it. My immediate reaction was, "Stupid boy!" but then I went to the counter to speaker to the customer.

"We'll have to ring your branch to get this authorised," I told him, "Do you have any form of identification?"

The man smiled and I became aware that most of the staff were falling about laughing and I couldn't understand why. Anyway, the man produced his driving licence so I could confirm his identity, and I told the cashier to telephone the account holding branch to make sure their customer had the necessary funds in his account.

I returned to my desk, and it was only then that one of the staff was kind enough to explain the reason for the hilarity. The mysterious stranger was none other than the current captain of the England football team and he had recently been transferred between two Premier League teams for an eight-figure sum. Of course, he had the funds in his account, his cheque was cashed, and he left the branch smiling. I must say he was very gracious in the way he chose to overlook my ignorance and I dare say he was able to get a few laughs in the changing room if he chose to tell the tale.

The mystery man is now a regular pundit on Match of the Day and each time I see him I have to smile at the memory of that day when he came face to face with probably the only man in England who didn't know who he was.

If you haven't already guessed, it was Alan Shearer!

William Porter.

Who was disinclined to wash

Please heed the tale of William Porter
Who absolutely hated water,
Especially when mixed with soap,
(With or without its useful rope.)
When bath time came around he would,
Even when head to foot in mud,
Inform his mother he was clean,
And make the most tremendous scene.

His parents vainly sought solutions
To organise the boy's ablutions.
They used a tranquiliser gun
To fire a dart into their son
Then placed him, drugged, inside the shower
And left him there for half an hour.
But this trick had to be rejected
When Social Services objected.

Psychiatrists were hired to probe
The cause of William's hydrophob-
-ia, but I am sad to say
They could not make it go away.
Would he grow out of it one day?

110

The answer, I'm afraid, was no,
He kept his fear of H_2O,
And masked his malodorous fumes
With aftershaves and cheap perfumes,
With extra strong deodorants,
And potent anti-perspirants.

This strategy would never work,
And very soon his social circle
Shrank 'til he was on his own,
Unclean and smelly, all alone.

So to avoid his fate you oughta,
Make use of cleansing soap and water
And not end up like him, I hope,
A hydrophobic misanthrope.

Little Sid.

Who was inclined to be led astray.

This is the tale of little Sid,
Who always did what others did,
For, having no mind of his own,
He followed where his friends had gone.
For instance, at the age of four
When show-off Jim, the boy next door,
Climbed up a tree, he thought, "Why not",
And followed him just like a shot.

Jim, at a height of fourteen feet,
To satisfy his great conceit,
Looked down, and hearing no applause,
Climbed down again and went indoors.
Which left Sid way out on a limb,
(A lesson which was lost on him.)

HEALTH

Gassy patient sets herself alight during laser surgery

By Matilda Battersby

A patient was left with serious burns when flatulence caused a fire during laser surgery.

The woman in her thirties, who has not been named, was undergoing a laser operation on the lower half of her body when she broke wind and the gas ignited.

The fire, at the Tokyo Medical University Hospital, in Japan, on 15 April this year left the patient with burns on her waist and legs.

"When the patient's intestinal gas leaked into the space of the operation, it ignited with the irradiation of the laser and the burning spread, eventually reaching the surgical drape and causing the fire," according to a report in Japanese daily newspaper *The Asahi Shimbun*.

Lasers are known to have the potential to ignite fires during surgery, with more than 100 cases reported in the US annually. They are a particular risk during airway surgery.

But fire during surgery remains "very uncommon", says Dr David West, of Veincentre Ltd. "Special care must be taken if there's fuel, such as methane, which can be in intestinal gas, or in farts, or in alcohol that is used to clean skin," he said.

Dr Harry Thompson, an anaesthetic registrar at Imperial Healthcare Anaesthetics, London, told i: "It's very rare."

113

Linda

Or the dangers of surgery they don't warn you about.

The Prologue

Now Linda knew she was a beauty,
She also thought it was her duty
To show it off at every chance,
From Southend to the south of France.
In her bikini or hot pants,
Her legs drew many a lustful glance.
But that was in her youthful prime
Now, with the ravages of time
Those legs that once were sure to please
Look like a piece of stilton cheese
And though her veins were varicose
She would not wear compression hose.
She thought she needed rather drastic
Action so she found a plastic
Surgeon who could put things right.
With skilful use of laser light
He'd make her legs pristine again,
Without discomfort or much pain.
He booked her in without delay -
Once he was sure that she could pay!

The Operation

Stripped bare from toes to shapely thighs
She lay before the surgeon's eyes,
And still preserved her modesty
With paper pants, provided free.
But, when the laser beam was started,
Unfortunately, Linda farted!
Her anal sphincter opened wide
And methane gas pent up inside
Burst out, and when this flatulence
Collided with the heat intense,
Provided by the laser light,
The gas was certain to ignite.
There was a most dramatic flash
The paper pants were burnt to ash
And poor old Linda's pubic hair
Went up in smoke and left her bare.

The Moral

Unsightly veins may not be nice,
They can be cured, but at a price,
A price as high as poor old Linda's
Her nether regions burned to cinders.

Lightning Source UK Ltd.
Milton Keynes UK
UKHW022110151222
414012UK00016B/455/J

9 781803 024295